SANTA MARIA IN TRASTEVERE

by

ROBERTO LUCIANI

FRATELLI PALOMBI EDITORI

ISBN 88-7621-322-8

Art direction: *Piergiorgio Maoloni*

Layout: *Legamon grafica e pubblicità*

Translation revised by: *Vivian Hewitt*

On the cover:
The church of Santa Maria in Trastevere by night

INDEX

SANTA MARIA IN TRASTEVERE

<table>
<tr><td>

1 Portico
2 Entrance vestibule
3 St. Francesca Romana's chapel
4 Crib chapel
5 Our Lady of the Sorrows chapel
6 St. Peter's chapel
7 Side entrance
8 Relics of various saints
9 Cardinal Armellini's funeral monument
10 The Winter Choir's (or Strada Cupa) chapel
11 Inscription Fons Olei
12 Ciborium
13 Apse vault
14 Altemps' chapel

</td><td>

15 Pietro Stefaneschi's sepulchral monument; Filippo d'Alençon's sepulchral monument and the altar of the Saints Philip and James
16 Vestibule of the sacristy
17 Sacristy
18 St. Jerome's chapel
19 Chapel of the Sacred Heart of Jesus
20 Tomb of Innocent II
21 St. Francis' chapel
22 Chapel of Our Lady of Divine Love
23 Baptistery chapel
24 Nave
25 Mino del Reame's ciborium

</td></tr>
</table>

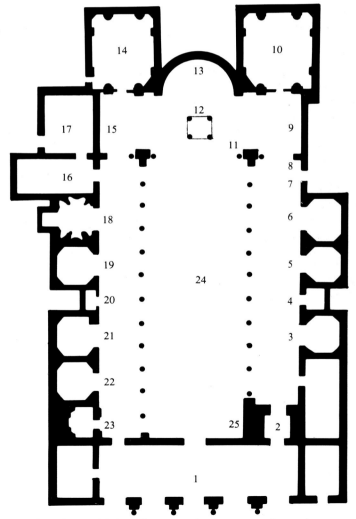

Notice.

The numbers between brackets which will appear in the text refer to the rooms

of this plan.

Preface

The Basilica of Santa Maria in Trastevere is clearly related to the history of the district of the same name and to the religious life of the city. The first Roman Christian communities, in fact, were born from the large Jewish colony — that counts many synagogues in Trastevere — and the episode that gave the name of ''Fons olei'' to the Basilica falls within this context.

Trastevere has always been alive with all the colours and contradictions of any port. On the one hand, it was the meeting point of people from all countries, with different languages and customs; on the other hand, strong social disparities marked the life of the district and its relationship with the rest of the city — of which it was only a suburb. Probably, this situation — dragging on for centuries — led Gregory the Great, native of this district, to associate the Gospel parable of the rich epulo and the poor Lazarus with the Basilica of Santa Maria in Trastevere, while he was reorganizing the Lenten ''stations''.

This Gospel heritage was more clearly expressed, many centuries later, by Francesca Romana. In fact, she used to go to the Basilica to pray and find the strength to serve the poor.

Then, when her parents forbade her to give away all she owned, she went begging for the poor, calling herself ''the poor of Trastevere''. She probably had in mind the example of St. Francis of Assisi, who chose to help lepers in this district.

Thus, the real meaning of the Basilica has to be found in this kind of episode: it has always been considered a house of prayer and welcome, and such meaning is stressed by the name it was given — the first church in Rome to be dedicated to the Mother of God — and by the ancient icon of Compassion that is venerated in it.

Trastevere is still today — though in a very different way — a sort of harbour district, and the Basilica still plays its old, and ever new, role of a house of prayer. The existence of the St. Aegidius' Community shows that the Gospel can still inspire prayer and charity.

We are very pleased to present this new guide for better understanding of this place of prayer whose origins go back to the very beginning of the Roman Christian Community itself.

Father
Vincenzo Paglia p.p.

The basilica and the piazza of Santa Maria in Trastevere in an engraving by G. Vasi (Photo by D'Onofrio).

INTRODUCTION

Santa Maria in Trastevere is, perhaps, the first Christian building opened in Rome and it is certainly the first one dedicated to devotion to the Virgin. It was founded by St. Callistus (217-222) and completed by St. Julius (341-352). Rebuilt by Innocent II (1130-1143) it was later decorated and restored, but the most substantial works were commissioned by Clement XI, who had the portico made (1702), and by Pius IX (1870).

Nevertheless, today's church, despite all the alterations, maintains the Romanesque stamp of the XII century. The motto engraved in the Basilica's coat of arms is *Fons Olei*, in the memory of a mineral oil spring which gushed out suddenly in 38 B.C. near the Roman *taberna meritoria*. The event was considered a miraculous announcement of Christ's birth. The spring is located to the right of the church's Presbytery.

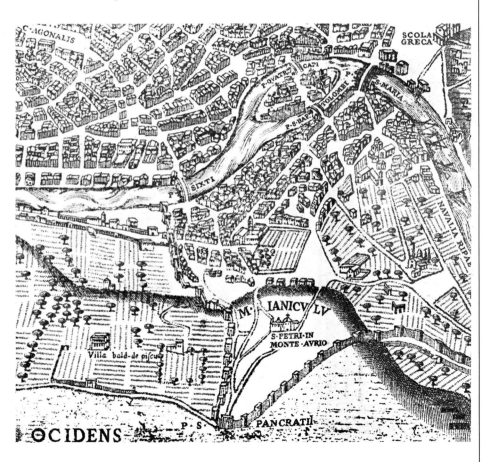

Francesco Paciotti, Plan of Rome, detail of Trastevere's area, printed by Antonio Lafrery, 1557 (Lanciani Collection).

9

BUILDING STAGES

In the year 38 B.C. an unusual event happened in Trastevere and was reported as follows: "at the taberna meritoria of Trastevere oil gushed out from the ground and kept running all day long without stopping, which means that the grace of God will come to the people" (St. Jerome's Chronicle, IV century).

Modern experts arrived at a correct interpretation of the event which had a volcanic origin: it was, in fact, a modest eruption of oil with its typical acrid odour. But the large number of Jews living in Trastevere at that time explained the happening as a sign of the Messiah's coming. Christians also, subsequently, had the same expectations: in fact, to them, the prodigious oil heralded Christ's grace that would save the people. That is why they started feeling the need to build a church, Santa Maria in Trastevere, on the site of the miracle at *taberna meritoria*, a place where *milites emeriti*, (retired and discharged soldiers) used to

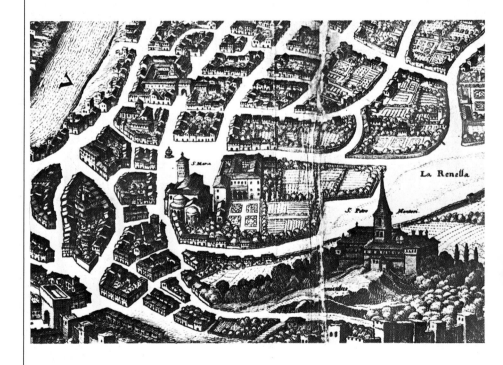

A. Tempesta, Plan of Rome, detail of Trastevere with the basilica of Santa Maria in Trastevere, 1593 (Lanciani Collection).

meet. The inscription *Fons Olei*, to the right of the church's presbitery, testifies to the sudden oil eruption.

It is known that a primitive place of worship (probably a *putealia*, a *domus* or a *memorial*) built by Pope St. Callistus (217-222) existed and was used by Trastevere's first Christian community.

In the same place, Pope Julius (337-352) later erected a huge church, the first in Rome consecrated to the Blessed Virgin. Some experts have suggested that there could be a connection between the oil and gas leakage and a *Fons Olei*, fountain of foul-smelling water. The fountain placed in Santa Maria in Trastevere's Piazza could have been already there, in a different form, since Roman times, fed by the unhealthy water Alsietina.

Nevertheless, another version close to the first one was also accepted in the search for Santa Maria in Trastevere's original site: at the *taberna meritoria* an *ecclesia domestica* was built first

The interior of the basilica reconstructed by Innocent II (1130-1143)
(Photo by Savio).

and then the church.

At about the end of the VI century the words *titulus Sanctae Mariae* appear for the first time in a document. It is known that under Hadrian I (772-795) the church was restored and enlarged by erecting the aisles. Pope Leo III (795-816) enriched it with furnishings and donations such as candelabra, censers and silk fabrics.

But it was Gregory IV (827-884) who undertook an *operosam decoramque reconstructionem*, a refined and elaborate decorative restoration. The large number of works: raising the presbytery; placement of the hight altar on top of the presbytery (originally it was at the bottom of the nave); ciborium covering for the altar; crypt excavation for the mortal remains of the martyrs Cornelius Callistus, Calepodius, Quirinus and Julius venerated by the faithful through the *fenestella confessionis* facing the east;

A capital and a base of the twenty-one granite's monolith columns distributed in the basilica.

The capital, classic Corinthian, of the Triumphal arch (Photo by Agostinucci).

installation of a Crib like the one in Santa Maria Maggiore (the actual Crib, in baroque style, is by Raguzzini); construction of a Monastery; placement of clergy's pews along the wall of the apse; elevation of the *Schola cantorum*; opening of a women's gallery. In 847-855 Leo IV restored the apse, while Benedict III (855-858) restored the portico, the baptistery, the sacristy and the apse and had coloured glass placed in the windows.

For a long period there was no maintenance following the reign of Benedict III, until Innocent II (1130-1143), who owned large estates in Trastevere, decided to rebuild the church completely. He found it in ruins: *Cum moles ruitura vetus foret* reads the inscription of the apse mosaics chosen by him. The Pope renewed the apse, added a transept, restored the wooden trussing and the Crib's chapel with the same IX century material. It took ten years to have the church completely renewed and

Domenichino, *Our Lady of Assumption,* table in bronze and copper
(Photo by Luciani).

materials from the Terme di Caracalla were used (columns, capitals, bases).

The most revolutionary innovation was Innocent II's addition of the transept. It is for this reason that the apse which was previously detached from the triumphal arch of the large nave jatted farther back from the posterior side of the transept. Innocent died before the church was completed but he left enough money to finish this ambitious operation. The church was consecrated by Alexander III (1159-1181) on May 22 of an unknown year and to this day the problem of the date remains. By then the basilica had acquired its present appearance: three aisles supported by twenty-one granite monolithic columns: ten to the right and eleven to the left. In addition, there are two columns supporting the nave's triumphal arch. These columns were taken from Terme di Caracalla and they

Altemps' chapel, vault frescoes.

have Ionic capitals with insignia of Egyptian cults, that are partially erased today.

The Triumphal arch's capitals and the tops of the columns at the end of the colonnade are Corinthian.

Between the two Popes Innocent II and Alexander III came Eugene III who erected the church's tower. The apse's gallery was enriched between 1290 and 1310 by Card. Bertoldo Stefaneschi with Pietro Cavallini's famous mosaics which represent salient events of the Virgin's life. They showed an artistic touch so advanced as to have influenced even Giotto. Vasari, in his "Biographies", mentioned some restorations by Bernardo Rossellino in Nicholas V's time (1447-1455). In 1489 there was a sacrilegious theft that deprived the Basilica of crucifixes, candelabra, patents and thuribles.

At the end of 1500, mainly during the pontificates of Sixtus

Nave's ceiling, in carved wood covered with pure gold, restored by Cardinal Pietro Aldobrandini in 1617.

V (1585-1590) and Clement VIII (1592-1605), many innovations were made: more specifically, Cardinal Marco Sittico Altemps built, on the left side of the apse, the Chapel of Madonna della Clemenza (Our Lady of Compassion) today Altemps's chapel; new chapels were opened; the *Schola cantorum* was demolished. On request of Cardinal Giulio Antonio Santori the transept's ceiling was completed and mosaics and decorations restored. The Altemps chapel was erected around 1548-85, as a memorial to the Council of Trent, by the titular cardinal of the Basilica and nephew of Pope Pius IV. The chapel was designed by the architect Martino Longhi. The vault and the walls were painted by Pasquale Cati of Iesi (1588). It housed the famous icon of the *Madonna della Clemenza*, wax-painted on three pine panels, probably of the VIII century.

The building transformations continued during 1600. In 1617, Cardinal Aldobrandini, renewed the ceiling of the nave, to Domenichino's design by placing a new one in carved wood covered with pure gold. The *Assunta* (Our Lady of the Assumption), a bronze and copper panel that dominates the centre, is also by Domenichino. The original is at the Louvre.

As time went by, many sculptures and sepulchral monuments enriched the basilica: the fifteenth century edicola-shaped ciborium, by Mino del Reame, a Gothic tabernacle placed between the sepulchral monuments of Cardinal Pietro Stefaneschi and Filippo d'Alençon; the sepulchral monuments of Cardinal Francesco Armellini (1524) and Roberto Altemps, duke of Gallese (end of XVI century) and many others. During the Baroque period the Coro d'inverno (Winter Choir) chapel or Strada Cupa — made to Domenichino's design (1581-1641) — was opened to the right of the transept. In 1624 a miraculous image of the Madonna, found in a Strada Cupa vineyard just below the Janiculum Hill was brought to the chapel: it is a fresco of the sixteenth century, by Perin del Vaga. In 1680 the Avila chapel, a marvellous piece of architecture by Antonio Gherardi, was opened and the final chapel arrangements completed. There are eleven in all; four in the right aisle, five in the left aisle and two, the largest, to the sides of the transept.

In 1702, under Clement XI, the portico by Carlo Fontana was added: five robust gates, divided by granite columns, are embellished at the top by four statues representing St. Callistus, St. Cornelius, St. Julius and St. Calepodius, Pius IX (1846-1878) entrusted the execution of major restoration works to the architect Virginio Vespignani. These works regarded the façade, the nave's floor which was lowered to reveal the column bases, the nave windows and the transept stairs.

THE EXTERIOR

The observation point is the evocative Piazza of Santa Maria in Trastevere. In addition to the basilicas's façade other buildings arranged round the square since the Baroque period are the Pizzirani palace, the Cavalieri palace, St. Callistus palace and the church's canonical house. The characteristic element, a main attraction for touristis and Romans alike is the *fountain* located in the middle of the square. It is one of the most ancient in Rome, believed erected under Augustus or during the pontificate of Hadrian I (772-795). There is evidence of this in an iconograph of the second half of the XV century. On an octagonal-shaped base stands a granite basin, also octagonal, in the centre of which there is the base with the Capitoline coat of arms from which a jet of water rises through the mouths of four wolves' heads. It falls into as many shells, and from there flows into the larger basin.

Outer façade (Photo by Anderson).

Typically Romanesque, the façade is the width of the three aisles. The higher part shows three large arched windows with horizontal shell borders and a tympanum; the lower part opens into three doorways, one for each aisle.

The front was decorated in the XIX century by Silverio Capparoni with frescos, now spoilt, which represent the *Saviour seated between seven candelabra with the Pontiff Restorer (Pius IX) kneeling at his feet and praying, with the symbols of the Four Evangelists*. The concave protective shell is designed to receive and protect the *Opus musivum* which shows the *Virgin Mary on the throne with Child*, and *two gift-bearers* at her feet with *two processions of Saints* holding lamps in their hands.

Initially the façade had three arched windows which were closed in the XVII century by Cardinal Pietro Aldobrandini, who opened one large square window in the middle, and a circular one in the tympanum.

The façade was re-designed by Carlo Fontana, who built the portico, re-built in its present form by the architect Vespignani who eliminated all the windows, both the originals recovered during the restoration and the existing ones, to open the three windows there are now. Between these Capparoni painted *four palms*, while *grazing sheep* are on the sides. They are plain works but they integrate the chromatic style of the front.

Mosaic of The Virgin Mary on the throne with child. In the middle, the Virgin on the throne nurses her child tenderly, two praying figures kneel at her feet, while the sides show a procession of ten Saintly Virgins. The mosaic was restored for the first time in 1466 during the pontificate of Nicholas V, and subsequently by Clement XI (1700-1721), Leo XII (1823-1829) and Pius IX (1846-1878). The upper edge of the mosaic, 12.50 m. long, with medallions depicting flowers and in the middle the mystical lamb, are all restored. Art historians are not in agreement about the author and the date of this glass tesserae, which is probably of the XIII century.

Another problem to be resolved is that regarding the procession of the Saints, some of whose lamps are lighted. Some scholars consider this scene to be the representation of the parable of *Vergini Sagge* (Wise Virgins) and of *Vergini Stolte* (Foolish Virgins) (Matthew, XXV, 1-13); for other scholars, the Virgins are all Saints that pay homage with the lighted lamp, symbol of fervent faith, while the lamps which are not lighted seem to be an error of restoration.

Mosaic showing Bethlehem. It is located in the higher part of the façade on the right wall. It represents Bethlehem on a yellow background. Recent research proved that is was a ''false mosaic'': the painting was designed to give an idea of the mosaic's tesserae (XII century). On the inclined wall, which covers the roof of the opposite aisle, there is a mosaic representing Jerusalem (XII century).

The Virgin on throne with Child,
mosaic, XII century (Photo by Anderson).

PORTICO AND EXTERNAL WALL

The portico is made of five round arches of classica form: the central three are framed by columns with Ionic capitals placed on square bases. Above the arch, a group of beams jutting towards the centre holds a terrace with transenna decorated by small columns. On the hand-rail we find four statues of Popes, promoters of the church, with raised hands and flowing vestments: St. Julius, St. Calepodius, St. Cornelius and St. Callistus, by Michele Maille, Lorenzo Ottoni, Vincenzo Felici and Giovanni Battista Théodon of the XVII century.

The portico, 25x9 meters, was built in 1702 by Carlo Fontana, to instructions by Clement XI (1700-1721) and replaced a colonnade. During this job, the pediment was stuccoed and shaped with architectonic structures and perspective "chiaroscuro" effects. The mosaic images of Virgins beside the *Madonna in trono* (Madona on the throne) were restored. The large iron gates are also by Fontana.

BELL TOWER

Of classical Romanesque style standing 20 m. tall, the lower part merges with the right salient of the church. From this point, four storeys emerge, and each of them is divided from the other by cornices and corbels. The lower storey has three blind arches. On the second storey, on the side looking on to the square, there is a clock with Roman numerals. The third storey has four blind arches with two slits in the central part. In the fourth there are trigores enclosed by two marble columns. In the main prospect, above the trigore there is a niche that houses a golden background mosaic representing *La Madonna col bambino* (Virgin Mary with Child). The top is eave-shaped with an ancient bell over it. All over the bell-tower there are ornamental red and green brickwork medallions (XII century).

BASILICA'S FLANK

The side of the basilica can be observed walking along the right outside wall towards the *Piazzetta St. Egidio*. The transept head with brick ornamentations of Innocent II's time (XII century) ends at the top with a cornice made of marble corbels, saw teeth and other sculpted bricks: the extra storey is mannerist. Slightly below, there is a tabernacle with two columns supporting a tympanum that once housed an image of the Saviour, perhaps of the XII century. At the sides two round windows closed in the sixteenth century. Above the projection of the present entrance one can also see the volumes of aisles with brick parapet and a series of projections, dated XVI-XVIII century, which house the chapels. At the top, the central part of the nave is plastered, while it is possible to distinguish the cornice brackets and brick friezes. From this point it is also possible to see the side and back of the tall bell-tower. By the oratory there is a small *cimitero dell'addolorata* (Our Lady of the Sorrows churchyard) or the Churchyard of the Souls in Purgatory; sacred dramatisations were held here in the past. The Oratory, erected in 1600 and restored in 1877, looks on to Via della Paglia. As we pass beyond the transept and enter the back courtyard, the apse, marked throughout by pilaster strips, can be admired.

The pilaster strips are jointed, at the top, by small arches with a cornice made of marble corbels and brickwork ornamentation.

Right side of the basilica
(Photo by Anderson).

THE PORTICO (1)

The atrium has many inscriptions, transennae, grave stones, sarcophaguses and sculptures wich all come from the same basilica, or were recovered by Marcantonio Boldetti in the XVII century from catacombs.

The narthex of the church is presently a small but important museum worthy of attention. There are important pictorial remains of previous ornamentation; the three front doors of the basilica, which have classical cornices of the imperial age, are also very interesting. Originally the three doors opened on the nave, but during the XVI century, Card. Altemps closed the smaller ones and opened other new doors which lead to the aisles.

The central door was opened as a "Holy Door" in the place

One of the sarcophaguses,
kept in the portico's atrium
(Photo by Agostinucci).

of "St. Pauls's Door", only for particular misfortunes like epidemics, Tiber floods, etc.

Among the funeral monuments, Miccinelli's and Giovanni da Lucca's grave-stones are worthy of mention; as regards sculptural frangments, we must mention the old basilica's plutei (IV century), the acanthus leaves, vines and berries, and particularly the fragments "Peacocks drinking from a vase" (IX century); one of the *cippi* contains Innocent II's ashes; among Christian sarcophaguses there is Giona's decorated with pastoral scenes and a lion, and that of Card. Campeggi's (1477-1554) ashes. We must not forget the XIII century statues, applied to the door's tympanum which come from Aleçon's monument, located inside the Church.

Transenna with floral themes
in bas-relief
(Photo by Agostinucci).

Cocceio's family sepulchral stone. Designed by Ambrosio and by Rufino, it shows the size and the location of the grave (III-IV century) and also the capital writing executed by the best tombstone sculptors.

Lunette-shaped sepulchral stone, with italics, on a couples's tomb to praise their exemplary lives. Beside the writing that occupies only the central part, there are two small palm trees which can be interpreted as hearts, symbols of love (IV century).

The beams of a pagan building is arranged in a rectangular frame that includes another one decorated with acanthus leaves. The central part shows many floral decorations (III-IV century).

Sepulchral gravestones of Larcio's family written in capital Actuaria, has dedications to the Mani gods and the veto, for posterity, on donating or selling the monument (IV century).

Celebrative stone (200x100 cm) inserted in a double frame

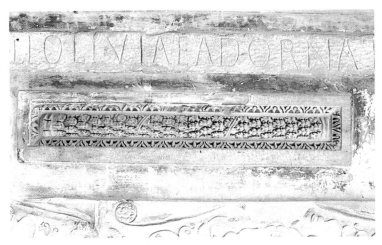

Trabeation of pagan building (Photo by Luciani).

including polychrome marbles. It was carved to celebrate the first anniversary of Santa Maria in Trastevere on September 23, 1702 during Clement XI's pontificate (XVIII century).

Transenna in bas-relief; with floral spiralling decorations. There is a rhombus in the middle (VIII century).

Marble Sepulchral stone (70x30 cm) dedicated to Claudia Titilia, Claudius' wife, who died when she was 22, one month and two days after marriage (IV century).

Celebrative stone, bearing witness to the particular custom of selling Papal indulgences. The income was donated to the Basilicas. The stone celebrates Leo XII who, for eight years, increased the material and moral assets of Santa Maria in Trastevere (XIX century).

Portali (portals). Before the Altemps restorations, all three portals opened towards the nave; this was an unusual arrangement due to the necessity of not disturbing the paving on the right where the church-tower is placed.

In the XVI century this precaution was infringed: two new doors were opened in the aisles and the old ones were walled. The ancient door posts were transferred to the new portals. The marble friezes with acanthus leaves were clamped in frames with linear moulds in the outside, in the inside, and under the architrave. The astragals and the chyma with acanthus leaves are arranged in two orders.

On the architrave's sides, there are smiling winged putti. The tympanums have mouldings of Ionic chyma dentils, arches and rises. In the larger central portals, above the wooden door of the XIX century, a round frame mould holds the mosaic representing the name of the Virgin's to whom the church is dedicated; the doorposts are III century.

Small statues representing the Redeemer, St. Peter, Saints and Virgins. Made of white marble 70 cm tall, placed above the portals' tympanyms, the statues come from Alençon's monument which is in the transept inside the church. The Redeemer in a pose of benediction holds an open book in his left hand, his face is framed by hair.

St. Peter holds the broken keys in his left hand, in his right hand a closed book, while the right forearm gathers his vestment.

Marble transenna with two peacocks drinking from a vase in the middle; they are leaning on two Greek crosses. At the end there are two floral decorations.

Fresco representing the *Madonna with child and St. Venceslao of Bohemia*, who died at the beginning of the X century; in warrior dress with ducal horn on his head, sword in one hand and standard in the other.

To the right side is the Angel of the Annunciation and before him, in the lower part, the gift-bringer. The Madonna, presented in warm colours, is under the customary canopy (XIV century).

Sepulchral gravestone, square-shape (60x60 cm), of which only one engraved amphora is left, to bear witness that the buried was baptised (V-VI century).

Sarcophagus. Sculptured in bas-relief in which a *pastoral scene* is represented. The three subjects are in focal perspective with their heads turned towards the same point (IV century).

Sepulchral gravestone with dedication not addressed to a particular defunct but to mankind, and particularly to youth to show them that death brings sadness, and that is why it is disliked by men; but at the end it brings resurrection to the soul in a blessed heavenly life. The initial cross symbolizes Christ's Passion (VII century).

Marble transenna sculptured, shows in the middle a trunk, perhaps representing a tree from where six circles for each wall rise; each circle is divided in four parts reminiscent of Byzantine motifs (VIII century).

Sepulchral gravestone, marble, rectangular-shaped, dedicated to Rennio's wife who lived for 13 years, 11 months and 23 days. The writing is capital Actuaria; the dedication ends with a dove carrying a small olive branch in its beak, an augury for the defunct (IV century).

Sepulchral gravestone, made of marble; it has three engraved Christian symbols: Christological monogram in one of its first examples; the doves symbolizing peace; a wine barrel for prosperity and fertility (IV century).

Sepulchral gravestone, rectangular (80x20 cm), dedicated to a little girl named Brumasia who died at the age of 1 year and 9 months. A heart — her parents' love for her — and a dove — for the peace of the little girl's soul — are added (IV century).

Sarcophagus, strigiled, with plate and dedication in capital Actuaria. The engraving tells us that Rufina Isceiasa dedicated the sepulchre to her beloved husband, perhaps Arnolfo Bentinoco (III-IV century).

Sepulchral gravestone dedicated to *Dionisia* who is sleeping — as marble engraving shows — waiting for her husband. We know from the written text that she lived for 20 years and 4 monts under the consulates of Lucius Cassius and Caius Dionis. The use of the one word *dormit* shows the tender-heartedness and sweetness of the person that ordered or who materially engraved the gravestone (IV century).

Sepulchral gravesone, fragmentary, (100x60) of Valerianus "Chartario". This means that the defunct was, professionally, either a paper-dealer or an archivist (IV century).

Sepulchral gravestone, belonging perhaps to a Greek, engraved on three lines, using the Greek alphabet (IV century).

Sepulchral gravestone, square (40x40 cm), in which only a working farmer is represented, without engraved words or dedication (IV century).

LEFT WALL

This fresco portrays the *Feast of the Annunciation*. The characters are in a room, in front of a once-gothic tabernacle which luminous rays penetrate. The Virgin Mary wears a blue mantle opening on a red dress; the characters on the right are the Angel and God coming out of the clouds (tangible representation of his descent to Earth). Two kneeling gift-bringers, a man wearing a dark coat and a woman covered with veil (XIV century).

The marble arch: sculptured in bas-relief; it might be the tabernacle's edicola. The arch is moulded with a wicker interlacing; on the upper part, to the sides of an interlacing knot, ther are two lilied figures; the higher cornice is curled in two opposite directions (XI century).

Marble bas-relief: the clothes of three characters seen in a focal perspective. Only in the central character is the torso frontal (V century).

Sepulchral gravestone: left part missing. On the right side there is a resting dove with an olive branch wishing peace to the defunct's soul. The writing is capital Actuaria, and it is dedicated to Marcus, who died 4 days before the October Kalends (IV century).

The tabernacle: stone-made, rather small (74x52x16), it has a tympanum and an architrave supported by two tortile cippi with Corinthian capitals moulded with two orders of acanthus leaves; all of this is placed on an Attic pedestal. It is ascribed to Vassalletto's school (XIII century).

COUNTER-FAÇADE (SOUTHERN WALL)

Cornice, jutting out, on which two puteals rise, on the second pilaster. The central strip, curving inwards, is sculpted with acanthus leaves, in a semicircle (VIII century).

Puteal sculpted in bas-relief, on the second pilaster. The central part features four animal heads, probably goats supporting a floral stylized festoon (VIII century).

Urn with no cover. At the corners, two bearded heads with goats' horns carrying a festoon with flowers and fruits. On the side an amphora among the branches of a shrub (III century).

Cippo that kept *Innocent II Papareschi's* ashes with tomb epigraph in Gothic writing dated 1148. Since the Pope died in 1143, that date may refer to the transfer of his remains from Santa Maria in Trastevere to the Lateran. In 1308 the remains were brought back to the Trasteverine church and the epigraph, even re-written, re-proposed the date of the first transfer instead of the date of death.

Taurino family sepulchral monument. The top part of the monument presents a classic tympanum leaning on two smooth pilaster strips with capital decorated from ovules. The pilaster strips contain an oval cornice sculpted with female figures and dedication (XVI century).

Marble tabernacle's cornice with epigraph. Nearly square-shaped, it forms the upper side to form a little fronton. There is a dedication epigraph engraved in Gothic letters (XIII-XIV century).

FLOOR

Sepulchral stone dedicated to Giuditta Forti from Rome, who died at 33 years, 5 months and 27 days, seven days from the August Kalends of 1829. Besides praising the young woman's virtues, the stone presents a Christological symbol preceeded by an A and followed by a Ω (XIX century).

Lucia Tremante's sepulchral stone, Roman, excellent wife of Domenico Colafranceschi and sweetest mother, who died when she was 28 years old. It follows the formula vouching for her hope in the resurrection of the flesh (XIX century).

Sepulchral stone with defunct's figure, sculpted in low-relief. In frontal position, he is dressed perhaps as a canonical; the face's features are non longer visible, only the pillow's traces remain at the sides. The right hand holds a cartouche, the left one a book, the arms, to give the effect of space, emerge slightly from the linear cornice of the stone (XV century).

27

The inside of the basilica with the nave and two aisles
(Photo by Anderson).

THE INTERIOR

The inside of the basilica has three aisles, divided by twenty-one granite pillars, from Terme di Caracalla, with Ionic and Corinthian capitals, on top of which there is a horizontal trabeation whose corbel cornice is made with fragments from ancient Roman buildings. The cosmatesque floor is XIX century; the lacunar ceiling is by Domenichino (1517), who also painted the *Assunta* (Our Lady of the Assumption), on copper, in the central octagon; the front of the triumphal arch, based on two huge red granite pillars with Corinthian capitals and acanthus leaves in the frieze, decorated with a fresco showing *The Virgin, Angels and the Patriarchs Noah and Moses* by L. Cochetti (1870). In the apse there are the famous mosaics showing the *Vita della Vergine* (Virgin's Life) by Cavallini, and those of Innocent's period (Mid XII century). Above the central doors, there are large windows painted by Antonio Moroni on Francesco Grandi's project, showing the *Saints Julius, Callistus and Cornelius.*

ENTRANCE VESTIBULE UNDERNEATH THE BELL-TOWER (2)

Marble transenna, sculpted with interlaced rectangles containing wheels, flowers and birds. The stone was sculpted for Gregory IV (827-844) who raised the apse's floor inserting some stairs and closing the presbytery area with marble transenna (IX century).

Marble transenna, sculpted with interlaced square motifs containing bunches of grapes and leaves (IX century).

Marble transenna, sculpted with St. Andrew's cross motif with umbons in a two-one-two sequence crossing. Hewn together with others of the same type during the restorations of the nineteenth century.

RIGHT AISLE

First chapel to the right, of St. Francesca Romana (3). It takes its name from a painting, dedicated to the Roman Saint, placed on the altar; the work is by Zanobi (1681-1767). The chapel, with central plan, and cupula covering on pendentives, was designed between 1721 and 1727, by Giacomo Recalcati; he was replaced, after his death in 1723, by Filippo Ferruzzi, and the chapel was completed by Francesco Ferrari. To the sides, *funeral monuments* by Francesco Ferrari: they belong to Cardinal G. Battista Bussi, with busts of G. Battista de' Rossi and of P. Francesco Bussi.

Second chapel to the right, of the Crib (4). Planned by Filippo Raguzzini, it has a Greek cross plan, and is covered by cupula on pendentives. The Neapolitan architect of the stuccoes also built the chapel, on Cardinal Antonio Fini's instructions, in the most ancient place of the basilica; erected by the Roman Gregory IV (827-844). It contains a *Nativity* by Stefano Parrocel, called ''the Roman'' (1696-1776).

Polychrome sculpture of *Our Lady of the Sorrows,* in the third chapel to the right.

Third chapel to the right, of dedicated to Our Lady of the Sorrows (5). The polychrome sculpture of *Our Lady of the Sorrows* is by a Bernini pupil, while the wooden *Cross* on the altar is of the XV century. It was placed at the nave's entrance and presents a near tranquil face that does not betray the drama of the event, which is shown in contrast by the musculature, stiff and tormented, of legs and arms.

Giuseppe Avio's bust († 1718) follows.

Fourth chapel to the right, St. Peter (6). It was built by Martino Longhi in 1583, at Muzia Velli's expense. On the altar *St. Peter receives the keys*, by Giuseppe Vasconio (XVII century); to the right *Francesco Longhi's funeral monument* († 1838), by Rinaldo Rinaldi. To the left side of the chapel the *cenotaph of Cardinal Pietro Marcellino Corradini* († 1743); in polychrome marble, it develops on a high curved base of ancient yellow and red marble, on top of which, on two lion's paw-shaped corbels, the black marble urn is placed. A Cardinal's bust, by Filippo della Valle (XVIII century) dominates the composition.

The *side entrance* to the church with Romanesque door follows. An interesting example of XII century sculpture with floral draped figurations; on one side we can note a Centaur with crossed shield; on high is the Virgin between two angels. On the left side of the door, in the nave, we can find some *Relics of various Saints* (8) inserted in a niche in the wall. Chains, a marble globe and black and red stones are kept in it. The chains are revered as matyrial instruments of some Saints; according to the legend, the globe was tied to St. Callistus's neck when he was thrown into the well of the church dedicated to him, and has a dedication of the veteran T. Cassius Miro to Jupiter of Damascus; some of the stones are Roman weights.

Memorial to Clement XII. Fundamentally, this is a simple marble inscribed tablet on which there is the text of a Bull of Clement XII Corsini (1730-1740) in memory of the restorations to the *Cappella del Presepe* (Chapel of the Crib) by Cardinal Antonio Fini who also erected a new altar. The Bull celebrates the consecration and concession of the Gregorian privilege (XVIII century).

Memorial to Benedict XIII. The tablet commemorates, with twentyfive fine capital letters, Vincenzo Maria Orsini's merits during his papacy (from 1724 to 1730, with the name of Benedict XII); it also commemorates his love for the Santa Maria in Trastevere church (XVIII century).

RIGHT TRANSEPT

The right side of the transept is covered by a *ceiling*, donated by Cardinal Giulio Antonio Santori, to the church with lacunars in golden wood, and blue and red background. In the central part a wooden group figuring the *Assunta portata in cielo da due angeli* (Virgin borne into Heaven by two angels). It underwent extensive restoration in 1872.

Immediately on the right we find the *funeral monument of Cardinal Armellini and his father Benvenuto* (9), which looks like a great politician with a wide and simple architectonic order. The Armellini monument is by Michelangelo Senese, pupil of Baldassarre Peruzzi, but until recently, it had been thought to be by Sansovino. This monument was erected by Cardinal Armellini for his father in 1524, when he was titular of the

The *Virgin borne into Heaven by two Angels,* wooden group placed on the transept's ceiling, XVII century.

32

Apse vault, mosaic of the XII century
(Photo by Vasari).

Coronation of the Virgin, apse mosaic,
1143, detail (Photo by Savio).

Apse vault, mosaic, detail.

P. Cavallini, *The Virgin and Child between Saints Peter and Paul,* XIII century.

P. Cavallini, *Nativity of the Virgin,* mosaic,
XIII century detail, (Photo by Savio).

P. Cavallini, *Annunciation of the Virgin*, mosaic,
XIII century, detail (Photo by Savio).

P. Cavallini, *The Adoration of the Magi*, mosaic,
XIII century, detail (Photo by Savio).

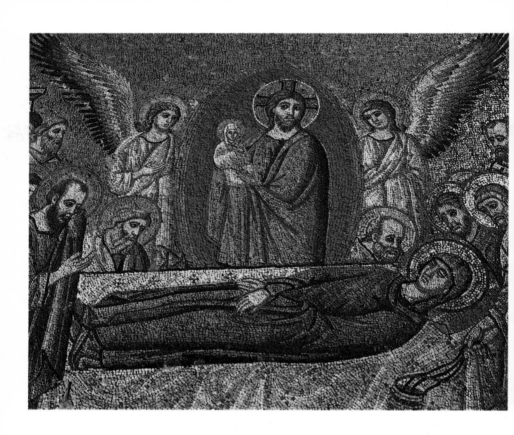

P. Cavallini, *The "dormitio" of Mary,* mosaic,
XIII century detail (Photo by Savio).

Copy of the VI-VII century icon showing
the *Madonna della Clemenza* (Our Lady of Mercy)
(Photo by Agostinucci).

P. Cati, *Pius IV promulgating the Papal bull Benedictus Deus,*
XVI century, Altemps' chapel (Photo by Vasari).

P. Cati, *Pius IV at the Council of Trent,*
fresco, XVI century, Altemps' chapel.

A. Ciampelli, *Angels with the symbols of the Mysteries of Mary,* fresco XVII century, choir (Photo by Vasari).

A. Ciampelli, *Angels with the symbols of the Mysteries of
Mary,* fresco XVII century, choir (Photo by Vasari).

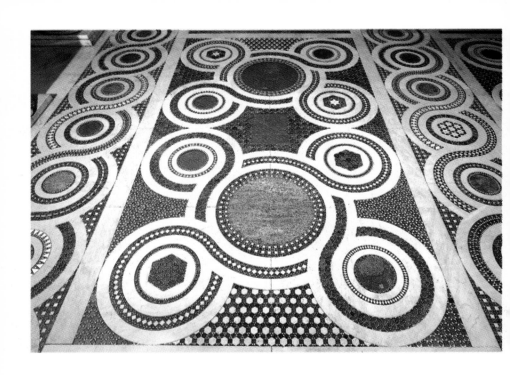

Cosmatesque floor, restored in XIX century
(Photo by Vasari).

Nave's interior
(Photo by Vasari).

basilica. It is composed of two sarcophaguses inserted between Corinthian capitals and channelled wall pillars. On the covers we find the figures of the Cardinal lying on one side with his head on his shoulder, and of Benvenuto Armellini with bust slightly raised. The important sepulchre shows some sculptures of *St. Lawrence and St. Francis and God the Father bestowing his Blessing* (on the main arch of the central niche); two figures of *the Virgin with Child*, bas-reliefs contained in clipeuses; two inscribed tablets (XVI century).

On the upper part of the monument, is the *Organ* donated by Cardinal Altemps. It has four channelled pilaster strips with Renaissance capitals; the façade pipes are divided into three spans with a central spire (late XVI century).

Painting showing *The prophet Isaiah*, fresco. This painting, together with the *David*, was an integral part of the late XVI

Funeral monument of Cardinal Armellini
(Photo by Anderson).

Mino del Reame, ciborium, XV century (Foto by Vasari).

century's decoration of the church, explicitly ordered by Marco Sittico Altemps, titular from 1580 to 1595. The prophet is shown in a mystical attitude, dressed in red with a green mantle. Painting featuring *Angelic musicians* (oil on canvas). The four paintings with the elegant figures of Angels playing the clarinet, the violoncello, the mandolin, the organ, the flute, etc., are attributed to Gaspare Celio (1571-1640). During the eighteenth century restorations the above works were almost completely repainted.

Coats of arms. On the lacunar ceiling — in gilded wood with a blue and red background (the general design is formed of three large squares, each inscribed with a Greek cross form) — we find, in the central part, the wood group showing *Our Lady of the Assumption* and, at the sides, two large wooden coats of arms. They are the coat of arms of Cardinal Santori who donated the transept's ceiling in 1596, and of Pope Pius IX, witnessing to the restoration works ordered in 1872.

Organ of the right transept,
various woods and metals, XVI century.

The construction of the chapel was begun in 1625 to host the image of the Virgin Mary that had been found in a street called Cupa, from which its name is derived. Two years later, it was given in patronage to the Cecchini family with the clause to finish the construction and to decorate it. Domenichino designed the architecture and the fresco decoration until 1630, when he left for Naples. The chapel walls are divided by fluted connecting rods with capitals and in the centre there are the heads of cherubin flanked by fruit festoons. At the top of the trabeation's high cornice there is a frieze, formed by eight panels, that is the connection point between the vault and the trabeation. The vault's main structure is formed by eight stucco telamons, represented supporting a composite capital that sustain the central panel. To the right wall, *St. John the Baptist*, attributed to Antonio Carracci; to the left, *Il riposo della fuga in Egitto* (Repose from the flight into Egypt) by Carlo Maratta.

Altar of the Strada Cupa chapel. It was built, on the instructions of Cardinal Henry Stuart, Duke of York, who was titular Cardinal of the Basilica from 1759 to 1761, by Zanobi Rossi, while Gaspare Sibilla was commissioned for the *Gloria degli Angeli* (Glory of the Angels). In late Baroque style with refined use of polychrome marble, the altar is marked by two green marble columns with gilt stuccoed Corinthian capitals. The central niche contains Perin del Vega's *Madonna di Strada Cupa*. Below the altar, is a black and white striped marble urn containing the relics of St. Alexander, St. Corona and St. Sabino.

Sculpture representing the *Glory of the Angels*. White marble Angels compose the altar display and surround the niche with the painted image of the Virgin. In the lower part and at the sides several cherubs appear among the clouds, while in the upper part two angels, partially covered by drapes, are holding an iron crown studded with stars. The author of this "aerial" decoration, dated 1762, is Gaspare Sibilla who, together with Bracci, created the important Benedictus XIV's statue in the Vatican (XVIII century).

Painting showing *St. John the Baptist*. It is an Antonio Carracci oil (1583-1589) on canvas painting (240x153 cm) that shows St. John the Baptist leaning on a rock and indicating the sky with his right hand. The figure appears static and rhetorical (XVII century).

Painting representing *Repose from the flight into Egypt*. This "oil", attributed to Carlo Maratta (or Maratti, 1625-1713) or to one of his pupils shows St. Joseph and St. Mary with the Holy Child on her knees. The Virgin is dressed in red covered by a blue mantle, and a wooded landscape forms the background (XVIII century).

Wooden choir of the Strada Cupa chapel. The wooden choir, situated along the two side walls has an uninterrupted back-rest divided into simple squares with well-shaped frames.

The coat of arms of Henry of York (XVIII century) is sculpted below the tympanum. The above-mentioned coat of arms is on the external tympanum of the chapel. Cardinal Henry of York was titular of Santa Maria in Trastevere from February 12, 1759 until July 13, 1761; subsequently he became commendatory of it until January 24, 1763. During this period he enriched the chapel with the right transept, of which he had the patronage, endowing it with a new altar, a choir and an iron gate that closes the chapel. The yellow, blue and Siena ochre coat of arms shows a wide shield with, at the base, a shell-form motif. A crown and a Cardinal's hat are placed on the upper part of the shield.

G. Sibilla,
Glory of the Angels. 1762.

Chapel of the Madonna
di Strada Cupa,
one of the eight stucco
telamons.

In the presbytery, in a marble enclosure partly restored in the XIX century with plutei (under the high altar there is the *Fenestella Confessionis*), on a step on the right (11) is the place, where in 38 B.C. oil sprang from the earth, *Fons Olei*, a presage to Christ's coming.

The ciborium (12) has been recomposed in the XIX century by Virginio Vespignani with ancient elements (porphyry columns and trabeation) and modern features ("tegurio"). The altar's case in purple is believed to have been built before the IX century.

On the right there is the *Candelabro pasquale* ascribed to Vassalletto's shop. It is a twisted marble column, moulded by four fasciae of polychrome mosaic thesserae, surmounted by a Corinthian capital (XIII century).

Ciborium, recomposed in the XIX century with ancient elements. To the right, Easter candelabrum (Photo by Anderson).

At the end of the presbytery, is the *Cattedra marmorea* made of two standing winged griffins which support a chair with a disc-shaped back. It is typical of the "cosmatesque" style (XII century).

The choir, semicircular, built in chestnut-wood with a walnut veneer, is composed of a row of high-backed chairs. It was built by the ebonist Giacomo Mammola in the XIX century, to a Vespignani project.

Above the choir's seats there are frescoes showing the *Angeli con i simboli dei Misteri di Maria* (Angels with the symbols of the Mysteries of Mary), by Agostino Ciampelli using tempera on the wall to depict Cardinal Alessandro de' Medici, who would become Leo XI. Every angel is bearing a mirror, a spray of roses and a well, a symbol of the Marian mysteries (1600).

P. Cavallini, *Nativity of the Virgin*, mosaic, XIII century.

Apse mosaic showing the *Incoronazione della Madonna* (Coronation of the Virgin). Built after the donor's death with vitreous tesserae, it still shows trace of classical elements. On a gold background Christ is in the middle and to his right there is the *Crowned Virgin* sitting on the same throne; in addition and reminiscent of an imperial epiphany, there is St. Peter, Pope Cornelius, the Martyr Calepodius, Pope Julius I (on the right); Pope St. Callistus, the deacon St. Laurence and Pope Innocent II with a model of the church in his hands (on the left).

Besides the obvious and common interpretation, this work could represent the *enthronement* of the Virgin as the Divine Son receives her in Heaven. In the open Book of God, the liturgy of the Assumption is written. So, the Virgin Mary is the symbol

P. Cavallini, *Annunciation of the Virgin,* mosaic, XIII century.

of the triumphant celestial Church, in antithesis with St. Peter (on Christ's right) who represents the Church on earth. This scene of Mary's preceeds, by more than a century, the one in the apse of Santa Maria Maggiore by Torriti; nevertheless, there are other interpretations. In the upper part there is the empyrean pavilion; in the fillet below the writing, six and six lambs (the twelve Apostles) leave Jerusalem and Bethlehem for the *Agnus Dei* who takes the sins of the world. Beside the apse, the arch mosaic features the *Prophets Isaiah and Jeremiah* who are unwinding the scroll with allusive verses to the Lord; the two birds in the cage symbolize Jesus confined for our sins. In the upper part we find the *Four symbols of the Evangelists*, the *Seven Candelabra of the Apocalypse* and the *Alpha and Omega cross*. There are two classical revocations in the arch's bases: genii elevate vases and a spray of flowers to which doves draw near (XII century).

Mosaic cycle showing *Stories of the Virgin's Life*. This is Pietro

P. Cavallini, *The adoration of the Magi,* mosaic, XIII century.

P. Cavallini, *Presentation of Jesus in the temple,* mosaic, XIII century.

Cavallini's (1250-1330) extraordinary work ordered by Bertoldo Stefaneschi "domicello" to the papal court. In the last century, the dedication bare writing with the author's name and the date was still visible: so there is no doubt that this is Cavallini work. The cycle begins from the left, on the wall near the apse with the scene of the *Natività della Vergine* (Virgin's Nativity), and continues in the vault with the *Annunciazione* (Annunciation), the *Nascita di Gesù* (Jesus' Nativity), the *Adorazione dei Magi* (Adoration of the Magi), the *Presentazione di Gesù al tempio* (Presentation of Jesus in the temple), the *Dormitio*. Every scene is commented by metric writing; under this narration fillet, in the middle, there is a votive plaque with the *Madonna tra i Santi Paolo e Pietro* (Virgin between St. Paul and St. Peter) and Cardinal *Bertoldo Stefaneschi* (XIII century) at her feet.

Mosaic showing the *Virgin's Nativity*. In a scene structured on distinct levels and characterized by curtains and vestments, St. Anne, sitting on the bed, assists in the bathing of the infant; near her two visitors offer food and beverages.

Mosaic showing the *Annunciation*. The attraction point of the scene is the huge throne that determines perspective; the Virgin sits with a book in her hand (it represents, with the vase, an element of French iconography), and receives the Angel's annunciation.

Mosaic showing *Jesus' Nativity*. Inside the grotto, Mary prostrate, listens to the Angels's annunciations to the shepherds. The lower part features St. Joseph, the *taberna Meritoria* in memory of the legend of *Fons Olei*, a young shepherd playing a fife and a dog turning its head towards the child.

Mosaic showing the *Adoration of the Magi*. In this fourth episode the three Magi, dressed in precious and embroidered clothes, bring their gifts to the Infant Jesus in the Virgin's arms in front of the throne. In the upper part to the left is a turreted town, probably Jerusalem.

Mosaic showing the *Presentation of Jesus in the temple*. Some architectural elements mark isolated characters; the scene seems blocked and represents Simeon with the Infant in his arms, the Virgin, St. Anne looking on, and St. Joseph offering white doves.

Mosaic showing the *"Dormitio" or Mary's transit*. To the left of the funeral bed, St. Paul cries at Mary's feet; to the right, between apostles and bishops, there is St. Peter with the Roman pallium and the incensory, while near the defunct, kneeling, is St. John; in the middle, between two angels, are the Redeemer and Mary's Soul. The composition of this last episode in based on horizontal and vertical lines: it is a further innovation with respect to Byzantine iconography.

Mosaic showing the *Virgin with Child between St. Peter, St. Paul and the Commissioner of the work*. The dedication panel of the cycle shows the Virgin with Child in a clipeus, between St. Peter and St. Paul. Bertoldo Stefaneschi, the work's commissioner, is portrayed kneeling and turned towards the Virgin. In the middle the Stefaneschi coat of arms.

Cavallini completed the important mosaic cycle before the paintings in St. Cecilia and after those of St. Paul's at about 1291. Although he keeps to Byzantines schemes, the artist's very personal interpretation of iconographies of the day is sometimes surprising, in his use of colour: he treats the mosaic as a fresco. Ghiberti — in his "Comentari" — wrote of Cavallini and his works in Santa Maria in Trastevere: "He was a supreme master; he painted all St. Cecilia in Trastevere with his own hand, also most of St. Chrysogony; he compiled mosaic stories in Santa Maria in Trastevere — six of which are in the main chapel. I would dare say I have never seen any better work of that kind".

P. Cavallini, *The Virgin and Child between Saints Peter and Paul and the Commissioner of the work,* XIII century.

In a higher position, located in the left aisle, there is the Altemps's Chapel. Commissioned by Cardinal Marco Sittico Altemps (Hoenems 1533-Rome 1595), son of Chiara Medici, the sister of Gian Angelo, Pope with the name of Pius IV, the construction began in 1584 directed by Martino Longhi the Elder. The decoration work began three years later and was carried out by Pasquale Cati, Pompeo dell'Abate and Stefano Fuerreri. The chapel's entrance, rectangular with a pavilion vault, is formed by a balustrade surmounted by a wrought iron railing; the writing *aperuit et clausit* (opened and closed) on the external cornice refers to Pius' IV work and to the Council of Trent. The walls are marked by palistrades that support an architrave on which there is a stucco frieze with Marian symbols,

Details of decoration of the Altemps' chapel (Photo by Luciani).

surmounted by a completely frescoed vault. The two huge side-frescoes describe two episodes in the lives of Pius IV and Cardinal Altemps (whose grave-stone is in the floor). The latter was titular of Santa Maria in Trastevere from December 5, 1580 until his death in 1595. On March 17 1593, the famous icon of the VII-VIII century, showing *Our Lady of Mercy*, the most venerable image of Mary, was moved from the *cappella ferrata* (ironshod chapel) — where it had been placed before — to the altar — where the ciborium is placed. The icon is presently at the National Institute for Restoration, and this is a copy.

Altar. Made by Martino Longhi the Elder at the same time as the chapel; in 1593 the icon showing *Our Lady of Mercy* was moved to the altar, while in 1715 the old wooden ciborium was replaced by the new one (see further). The altar has in the lower part, an alabaster frontal with a cross in the middle, supporting two Corinthian capital columns; these columns bear architrave with a three-cornered tympanum (XVI century).

Ciborium. Built with various and precious marbles, it has a cylindrical shape and is surrounded by six Corinthian capital columns that support an architrave with a three-cornered tympanum. The ribbed dome supports a lantern with a sphere surmounted by a cross. Planned by Girolamo Odam, it was built by the stone-cutter Giovanni Battista Luraghi (XVIII century).

Painting showing *Pius at the Council of Trent*. It is a huge fresco (375x350 cm) by Pasquale Cati, a pupil of Cavalier d'Arpino, showing the triumphant *Ecclesia* leaning a hand on St. Peter's unfinished dome, while in the background a session of the Council of Trent is under way (XVI century).

Painting showing *Pius IV the "Benedictus Deus" Bull*. This large

fresco, placed in front of the previously described work and by the same artist, shows the Pope proclaiming the Bull of January 26, 1564 approving the Acts of the Council.

Cycles of frescoes showing *Episodes in the Virgin's life*. The vault's central oval, with the Assumption, is surrounded by four mirrors showing episodes in the Virgin Mary's life, alternated with four ovals showing the Evangelists. Above the windows there are four polygonal mirrors showing episodes from the life of Jesus and the Virgin. The author is Pasquale Cati (late XVI century).

Painting showing *The Assumption*. In the oval of the vault the fresco, by Pasquale Cati, shows Our Lady of the Assumption surrounded by cherubs above the Apostles standing around the empty sepulchre.

Painting showing *The Virgin Mary with the Holy Child and*

P. Cati, *Pius IV promulgating the Papal bull Benedictus Deus,* XVI century, detail (Photo by Agostinucci).

Altemps chapel (Photo by Vasari).

St. Callistus, the Pope. This painting, placed on the altar, reflects Our Lady of Mercy, in terms of iconographic schemes. It shows the Virgin, in a red dress, sitting with the Holy Child on her knees, two angels by her side and possibly St. Callistus at her feet (XVIII century).

Medici's coat of arms. It is, more precisely, the coat of arms of Angelo Medici, who became Pope with the name of Pius IV (1559-1565) and whose life and work have been repeatedly described in the chapel's iconographic project. The coat of arms is located on the tympanum of the entrance door; it is in white stucco, outlined in gold, surmounted by a triple crown held by two angels (late XVI century).

To the left of the apse, there is the *Sepulchral monument of Robert Altemps*, captain of the Papal troops at Avignon and Duca di Gallese, a fiefdom he won for his faithfulness to Sixtus V's policy. The tomb, ordered by his widow Cornelia Orsini, has in its lower part a bas-relief with weapons and classical emblems. Above, the black tombstone and the half-length figure of the young defunct are placed into a shell-shaped clipeus surrounded by the triumphal crown, recently attributed to Nicolas Mostaert. On the tympanum, broken in the middle, amid the family's coat of arms there are the statues of Victory and Minerva, by Giovenni Antonio Paracca, called the "Valsoldo". This sepulchre represents the artistic expression of the late "Cinquecento" (sixteenth century), with the marble's polychromy

Roberto Altemps'
sepulchral monument, XVI century
(Photo by Anderson).

47

skillfully alternated and the spatial distribution of the figures (late XVI century).

Near the left transept's left wall there is the *Sepulchral Monument of Pietro Stefaneschi* (1417) (15), member of a famous Trastevere family. The tomb, signed by "Magister Paulus", is composed of a statue showing the defunct laid out and dressed in a red-edged tunic; below it there is an epigraph in Gothic letters with four twisted columns and two weapons wrapped in a red and silver cloth at the sides.

The face of this Prince of the Church has fine features, with a sharp nose and angular cheek-bones, adding a certain "regality" to the young figure (XV century).

His features are quite different from those of his French colleague at the other side of the altar. It is the *Sepulchral Monument of Filippo d'Alençon* (✝ 1397) of a French noble family; he

Pietro Stefaneschi's
sepulchral monument, XV century
(Photo by Anderson).

was titular of Santa Maria in Trastevere and then bishop of Ostia. Made of white marble, the monument shows the defunct lying in pontifical vestments; below it, there is an haut-relief showing the *Dormitio Virginis*; above it, a large cornice, this is typical of the Roman Trecento (fourteenth century), the cardinal is wearing pontifical vestments, with mitre and embroideries, the chasuble has painted embroideries on the shoulder (XV century).

The Sepulchre, divided in two parts, had been moved by Cardinal Altemps in order to relieve the transept, as we can see from the memorial tablet now backing the Gothic aedicula surmounting the *Altar dedicated to St. Philip and St. James*. The work, placed between the Stefaneschi and the d'Alençon Sepulchres, is composed of a Gothic aedicula held by two twisted columns with golden capitals; in the middle there is a canvas showing the martyrdom of St. Philip and St. James; in the lunette, in bas-relief, the representation of a cardinal praying before Our Lady of the Assumption. There are six statuettes on the pinnacles and the table is made of a slab embossed with a cross on which a memorial tablet is placed (XIV-XV century).

An *Organ*, contained in a monumental case covered with gilt decorations and carvings, is placed against the wall. It was built by M. Charles-Mutin, a disciple of Aristide Cavaillè, and it has a three-part perspective each with a set of pipes (XIX century).

Walking along the left aisle, it is possible to enter — through a door to the right — a room preceeding the Sacristy, or walk along the above-mentioned aisle.

Altar dedicated
to Saints Philip and James, detail
of the slab embossed with a cross.

Memorial sepulchre of Alessandro Lazzarini, dean of the Basilica, who died during Gregory XVI's papacy, at the age of seventy. The sepulchre, a green marble pyramid with metal lions lying down and a medallion with a profile of the defunct, had been erected by Notary Pietro Brocardo, a friend of Lazzarini's (XIX century).

Memorial sepulchre of Gaetano Bottari. Devoted to the study and diffusion of culture, he was prefect of the Vatican library and died in 1775 at the age of eighty-six. The pyramidal sepulchre has, in the lower part, a memorial plaque by Pietro Pogginio; above it, there is a green and white striped marble pyramid with a medallion with a portrait of the defunct in the middle (XVIII century).

Fifth chapel to the left, of St. Jerome (18). The architect who designed this elaborate chapel,(dedicated to St. Jerome by the Avila family), is withouth doubt Antonio Gherardi , who also did the painting, portraying a very colourful St. Jerome (1686). The originality is in the multilinear plan of the surroundings, in the perspective of the altar, in the dome, where the angels hold an aerial perspective of colonnades: here we have an original fusion of architecture, perspective and ornamental plastic. The Sepulchres of Diego and Gerolamo Avila are by Antonio Gherardi as well (XVII century).

Fourth chapel to the left, of the Sacred Heart of Jesus (19). Its name comes from Francesco Gagliardi's *Sacred Heart*, located on the altar. This chapel, already dedicatad to St. John the Baptist, was ceded to Marcantonio della Porta in 1602; the painting portraying this Saint is in the *chapel of the Winter Choir*.

Tomb of Innocent II (20). In heavy neo-classical style, this tomb in Carrara marble was designed by Vespignani. A sarcophagus, surmounted by a tympanum cover, lies on a plinth flanked by two palistrades (XIX century).

Third chapel to the left, of St. Francis (21). On the altar, *St. Francis* bearing the Stigmata by Ferraù Fenzoni who is also supposed to be the author of the left lunette and of the frescoes showing *God the Father with the Angels*. The chapel had been purchased, in 1591, by Francesco Ardizi and restored by Pietro Camporese, who closed it off with a banister.

Second chapel to the left, of Our Lady of Divine Love (22), founded by Mario Spinosa (1618) and formerly dedicated to St. Marius and St. Callistus; there is a modern copy of the *Image of the Castel Leva* on the altar. Marcantonio Boldetti's memorial epigraph (1749) is located on the external pilaster of this chapel.

First chapel to the left, of the Baptistry (23). Cardinal Francesco Antonio Fini through Filippo Raguzzini (1680-1771), had it changed into its present form. The octagonal-plan room is built over a Roman *Domus*, discovered in 1920, which had, at the moment of the discovery, well preserved walls and traces of green and red striped paintings. Originally, in the place of the Baptistry's chapel there was a chapel dedicated to the Archangel Michael: Francesca Bussa — S. Francesca Romana — used to pray there, and she also had several visions there.

Painting showing *Our Lady with the Holy Child*. This fresco is part of a larger painting by an unknown artist. The Virgin, wearing a red dress and a blue mantle studded with stars, is sitting on a throne, holding the Child bestowing His blessing.

Memorial sepulchre of Anna Maria De Ferris. This work was made of precious marbles such as antique green, granite and alabaster. From the top, we find a tympanum, shattered in the middle, lying on two palistrades which frame an epigraph (XVII century).

Fifth chapel to the left,
of St. Jerome, by A. Gherardi, detail of the dome
(Photo by Anderson).

51

"Cosmatesque" floor. Total reconstruction deriving from the last century's restorations and imitating the "cosmateque" technique and style. It is divided into three rectangular compartments, each of them containing five interlocked circles, bordered by rows of circles that cross each other perpendicularly. Some fragments of the medieval floor are still visible in the transept, between the altar and the bishop's chair (XIX century).

Ceiling. It is a lacunar ceiling by Domenichino (Domenico Zampieri, 1580-1641). It was ordered by Cardinal Pietro Aldobrandini, Chamberlain of the Basilica in 1617, whose memory is celebrated in a capital lettered inscription on a golden background and in a coat of arms divided by indented strips with six stars at the sides and surmounted by a cardinal's hat.

C. Fracassini, *St. Francesca Romana,* XIX century.

Painting showing *Our Lady of the Assumption in Glory*, again by Domenichino. Placed in the central octagon of the nave's ceiling, it shows the Virgin with open arms, wearing a red and blue dress, and surrounded by diminutive angels (XVII century).

Cycle of paintings showing the *Saints*. Frescoes on the nave's walls during the restoration works ordered by Pius IX in 1865-66; the technique of execution of the sixteen figures required a mosaic-like background to harmonize them with the rest of the church wall decorations.

Among them, we find *St. Bridget* with a cross in her hands (by Cesare Mariani); *St. Marius* with the palm of martyrdom (by Enrico Bartolomei); *St. Cecily* receiving a crown from a cherubin (by Marcello Sozzi); *St. Rufina*, covered by a brown mantle (by Luigi Fontana); *St. Francesca Romana* by the side of a young angel (by Cesare Fracassini); St. Gregory holding in his hand a model of the church (by Enrico Chiari) (XIX century).

Pulpito: a wooden canopy, engraved and decorated, against a column (XVIII century).

Ciborium, by Mino del Reame (25), made in golden travertine marble, signed ''opus Mini'', that is to say Mino del Reame, a pupil of Mino da Fiesole. Within pilaster strips, decorated with vegetal symbols, there is a classical architectural perspective in which five angels are at the sides of the door with the inscription ''Olea Sancta''. It is one of the best sculptural works of the Quattrocento (fifteenth century) in Rome, where all the classical elements and all the artifices of the ''sticciato'' (a kind of bas-relief) technique are utilized. The general architecture is *aedicula-like*, with pilasters, supporting an architrave. The dove of the Holy Spirit descends from the higher tympanum (XV century).

Aquatic birds, mosaic,
coloured stones tesserae, I century A.D.

THE OTHER ROOMS

VESTIBULE OF THE SACRISTY (16)

Mosaic showing *Aquatic birds*. According to some scholars, this mosaic — made of little tesserae of hard stone — comes from a classical temple of Palestrina, where it was used as the central part or as a symbol of a larger mosaic. It is finely worked in the Alexandrine style of the late Augustan Age (I century A.D.).

Mosaic showing the *Fluvial scene*. This mosaic, as the previous one, comes from Palestrina, the old Preneste, a city 40 km from Rome, where it was used as a symbol of a *"pavimentum tassellatum"*, worked with *"opus vermiculatum"*. The small tesserae of a few millimetres have been placed using many shades and tonalities of brown and green (I century A.D.).

Relief showing *The Visitation*. In terracotta, attributed to Francesco Grassia, called ''il Siciliano'', a Baroque artist, it shows the episode of the Visitation, with the Virgin, St. Elizabeth and other characters (XVIII century).

Relief showing the *Resurrection of the Dead*. In terracotta; its plan has long been attributed to Bernini, while modern critics affirm that the bas-relief is the work of Nicola Sale, even though Bernini retouched it. It is the bas-relief that adorns Francesco de Raymondi's funeral monument in the chapel of St. Peter in Montorio. It has a trapezoidal shape and shows the moment of the Resurrection of the Dead during the Last Judgment (XVII century).

Ewer. In marble, it consists of a small sarcophagus with a clipeus with the defunct's bust in the middle, embedded between two channelled pilaster strips wihich support an architrave with the coat of arms of Cardinal Stefano Nardini, once archbishop of Milan. He was titular of the Basilica in 1483, and restored the sacristy and adjoining rooms.

SACRISTY (17)

The restoration of the Sacristy was begun at the beginning of the XVIII century, by architect Bizzaccheri (Rome, 1655-1721) who also obtained a precious niche from it, adorned with stuccoes forming vegetable shoots interlaced with a ribbon. Along the walls there are the *armadi* (cabinets) with doors numbered up to XII, according to the number of canons. This work, in classical style, was also by Bizzaccheri (XVIII century).

Besides the above-described works there are many liturgical "objects" in the sacristy: candelabra, incense-boat, silver and brass chalices, pissids, "palmatori", aspergillums, plates, embossed thuribles, ampullae and trays.

Fresco showing *St. Callistus*. In the shape of an oval, it is enclosed in a stucco cornice. The Saint is shown with the palm of martyrdom in his hand, and the leaden disk placed around his neck when he was thrown into the well (XVII century).

Painting showing the *Virgin and Child*. Attributed to Benedetto Diana, it shows the Virgin holding the naked Child on her knees; on the background, a hilly landscape, with trees and two battlements (XV century).

Painting showing *The Virgin on the throne and Child*. By an anonymous painter from Viterbo. The Virgin is sitting on a throne with dossal held by twisted columns and decorated with "cosmatesque" designs; the Commissioner of the work is kneeling at her feet.

Painting showing *The Virgin Mary on the throne with the Holy Child and St. Sebastian and St. Roche*. This work, erroneously attributed to the Perugino, was by Mariano di Ser Austerio. The Virgin, surrounded by cherubs, is bathed in an almond-shaped light; the Holy Child is grasping her blue mantle while St. Sebastian and St. Roche are standing next to her, in a marshy landscape (XVI century).

Sketch showing *The Assumption*. This work was made in terracotta, by Francesco Grassia, called "il Siciliano". An Angelo with floating garments announces to Mary, who is kneeling to the right, her coming maternity (XVII century).

EXTERNAL COURTYARD

There are several marble fragments, mostly from transennae and frames — and especially from the Renaissance period — such as fragments of rounded arches and architraves that were walled up in the court-yard after the church's restoration by Vespignani (1866-1874). There are also travertine cippi (one of them with an inscription asking for offerings for the reconstruction of the church); a holy-water wall basin with raised edge; a broken travertine spiral column from the first construction of the Basilica, in the XII century, during Innocent II's pontificate; and an architectural frieze of the XVII century, in the form of a large shell.

Painting showing *St. Cecily's death*. The scene of the prostrate Saint helped by two women is dominated by Christ and a cherubin who is bringing her a crown (XVII century).

The parchment has, in the middle, an inscription with the Basilica's story, and at the sides — on a wide margin — the characters and episode involved. This parchment, together with one bearing the papal note on the institution of the Society of the Sacraments that is also kept in this hall of relics, was ordered by Thomas Treter. He was one of Santa Maria in Trastevere's canons, who came from Poland with Cardinal Osio, and devoted his life to study and to the restoration of Cardinal Altemps'Basilica (XVI century).

Painting showing *St. Frederick attacked by two rogues*. This canvas

Mariano di Ser Austerio,
Virgin Mary on the throne with Child and Saints Sebastian and Rochus, oil on panel, XVI century.

by Giacinto Brandi portrays the Saint, dressed in his episcopal vestments, at the very moment when he is about to be assaulted by the rogues. An angel emerges from a cloud and offers him the palm of martyrdom (XVII century).

Painting showing *Justice, the Expulsion of Adam and Eve, Judith with Holopherne's head*. It is a peculiar painting showing several allegorical episodes (XVI-XVII century).

Painting showing the *Decoration of the Basilica of Santa Maria in Trastevere*. It serves as one of the nave's walls and it is probably by one of the painters who, directed by Vespignani, restored the building in 1868 (XIX century).

Painting showing *St. John Nepomuceno*. Five stars — which

Coffer-shaped brass shrine, XVIII century.

are his traditional iconographic attribute — are painted in the background of the meditating Saint (XVII century).

Painting showing *Cain and Abel*. The work is clearly influenced by the Cortonesque school and shows Cain, covered with skins, leaning on the lifeless Abel. In the background a horrified shepherd runs away towards a bare landscape (XVII century). In the hall of relics we can also find crucifixes, candelabra, monstrances, shrine bust (St. Blaise, the bishop, and St. Apollonia). Shrines of various forms — such as temple reliquaries, cylindrical urns, coffer-shaped urns, oval-cup and cross-like shrines — and of different materials — such as embossed brass, gilded wood and silver — are usually kept in this hall.

Coat of arms of Cardinal Francesco Antonio Fini, titular of the basilica from 1738 to 1743, pure gold thread on silk, Roman manufacture, XVIII century.

VESTMENTS HALL

In this room we can find many excellent products of Roman manufacture, made between the XVI and the XIX century. Some examples: a chasuble in silk brocade, tunics with sumptuous golden embroideries, coats of arms, stoles, copes, frontals with floral decorations and leafworks.

CHAPTER-HOUSE

Cycle of paintings of the Evangelists and Angels with the Symbols of the Passion. Erroneously attributed to Giulio Pippi, called Giulio Romano, a pupil of Raffaello Sanzio. The paintings decorated the inside of a small wooden dome that was used to keep the relics and was placed on the confession. The trapezoidal paintings of the Evangelists, that have been detached and put on canvas, show *St. Matthew* writing, with an angel; *St. John Evangelist* with the eagle; *St. Mark* in the act of reading; *St. Luke* with the bull. The eight paintings of the *Angels with the Symbols of the Passion* are all triangular, detached and put on canvas, and have an identical scheme: four small angel heads surround a central angel holding one of the symbols of Christ's Passion, (the Cross, the Stick with the Sponge and the Whip, the Sacred Staircase, the Crown of Thorns, the Instruments of the Crucifixion and the Lance, the Flogging Column, etc.) (XVI century).

Restoration work in the basilica of Santa Maria in Trastevere began in 1983 and is still going on. Priority has been given to the work needed to ensure the conservation of the basilica itself. So far, the wooden structure of the roof has been overhauled, strengthened and restored and the surface covering rebuilt to stop the decay caused by the filtering through of rain. Geological tests, the measuring of cracks and unevenness, traditional and photographic surveys have also been undertaken.

Tests made between 1983 and 1985 measured the extent of the damage and carefully monitored the overall cracking.

The damage, which involved both the interior and exterior of the building, was particularly evident on the triumphal arch, in the right chapel of the transept (the Strada Cupa chapel) near the portico of the entrance, near the first chapel on the left and on the main façade. A geodetic survey has also revealed recurrent variations in the phreatic stratum below.

The results have shown that while the unevenness is not overall, there is a generalized decay due to weather conditions, and to different isolated incidents, such as the placing of unevenly distributed loads on the wall structures, alterations and extensions the building has undergone and so on; in particular, the wide extense of roofing (ca. 2,500 mq.) and the span of the wooden trusses create an uneven distribution of weight on the walls beneath.

As a result of these studies, a project of static consolidation has been devised which takes into account the architectonic whole and, without creating excessive rigidity aims, in as much as it is possible, to give the walls back their static balance and original solidity. This works consists principally in suturing and binding the disconnecte walls, providing compensation with a suitable type of mortar where the damage is extensive, overhauling, strengthening and repairing of the wooden structures of the roof covering and the joining of the wall mass to the top of the masonry itself.

Work started along the left aisle and adjoining chapels, and continued with the transept chapels and the repairing of the lead covering of the apse vault.

The most complex phase, which comprises the repairs to the coverings, is being undertaken with current financing: restoration of the transept and nave, each considerably damaged, both at the keystone and at the back of the triumphal arch.

Surveys carried out revealed the need to remove from the arch itself the stress deriving from the weight of the transept trusses that rested upon it.

This was obtained by placing an iron truss above the triumphal arch, at the height of the nave roofing. This was placed, bridge-like, on the suitably strengthened end walls of the nave.

After removing the roof-tiles and the concrete layer, the wooden structures and tops of the trusses were coated in sheet metal then screwed on the the above iron structure with the aid of metal bars.

Alongside the restoration of the wall structures, work also started on the wooden lacunar ceiling of the transept and nave. The coffers were fixed to the trusses above by means of wooden and iron tie-beams, the structure of which is extrememly light and appears only at the distance of the visitor to be powerful. Renovation work consisted in the removal of dust and débris from the upper part of the coffers, the checking, repairing and strengthening of the hooks linking the trusses above, and the restoration of the decorated surface. Also undertaken were emergency measures followed by the restoration of the wall decorations and paintings of the main façade of the church. Finally, the four statues above the entrance portico were restored.

The renewal of the coverings of the right aisle and its chapels will end the process of roof-repair.

This restoration programme, including research and surveys has been carried out by the Soprintendenza per i Beni Ambientali e Architettonici del Lazio.

Rome, December 1990.

Architects

Paola Degni, Elvira Cajano

BIBLIOGRAPHY

C. CECCHELLI, *S. Maria in Trastevere*, Roma, 1933.

C. BRANDI-C. BERTELLI, *Il restauro della Madonna della Clemenza*, "Bollettino dell'Istituto Centrale del Restauro", 1960, nn. 41-44 1964).

G. MATTHIAE, *Mosaici medioevali delle chiese di Roma*, 1967, pp. 367-378, 305-314, 421-222.

R.E. SPEAR, *The Cappella della Strada Cupa: a Forgotten Domenichino Chapel*, "The Burlington Magazine", III, 1969, n. 790, pp. 12-13.

P. HETHERINGTON, *The Mosaics of Pietro Cavallini in Santa Maria in Trastevere*, "Journal of the Warburg and Courthauld Institutes", 33, 1970, pp. 84-106.

R. KRAUTHEIMER, S. CORBETT, W. FRANKL, *Corpus Basilicarum Christianarum Romae*, Le Basiliche paleocristiane di Roma (sec. IV-IX), vol. III, Città del Vaticano, 1971, pp. 65-71.

G. BERTELLI, *Una pianta inedita della chiesa alto-medievale di S. Maria in Trastevere*, "Bollettino d'Arte", s. 5, 59, 1974, 3-4, (176), pp. 137-160.

D. KINNEY, *S. Maria in Trastevere from its Founding to 1215*, New York, 1975.

H. FRIEDEL, *Die Cappella Altemps in Santa Maria in Trastevere*, "Römisches Jahrbuch für Kunstgeschichte", 17, 1978, pp. 89-123.

R. LUCIANI-W. POCINO, *Roma*, Guide De Agostini, Novara, 1986, pp. 236-137.

Finito di stampare
nel mese di giugno 1993
presso gli stabilimenti delle
Arti Grafiche Fratelli Palombi srl
Via dei Gracchi 183
00192 Roma